SELLING A PRACTICE

Straightforward Answers
to Tough Questions

ROY R. BRAATZ

First U.S. Edition 2008

ISBN: 978-0-9800458-9-5 Hardcover

This publication is designed to provide accurate and authoritative information in regard to the subject matter covered. It is sold with the understanding that the publisher is not engaged in rendering legal or accounting services. If legal advice or other expert assistance is required, the services of a competent professional person should be sought.

The author can be reached at: roy@questbrokers.com

Contents

Planning Questions

Broker Questions: It's impossible to answer these common broker questions without some bias. I've done my best. They should at least give some food for thought when engaging a broker.

Questions Buyers Ask: These questions will interest many sellers.

INTRODUCTION

Nothing annoys me more than someone publishing a book that is a poorly disguised sales pitch for a company's services, when the content of the book is neither useful nor practical. I hope this book is genuinely of value and objective in its presentation— that it encourages more questions that need answers. If it leads to a reader's interest in my services it would be the highest compliment.

The information contained herein represents years of experience. The result of this experience is a finely tuned process for selling tax and accounting practices. When properly performed it involves asking the right questions at the right time.

The book was written for practice owners who gross $2 million in revenue or less a year. Others may also find this book beneficial, such as owners who gross more than $2 million in revenue a year or owners of a firm with multiple partners. However, it may not answer all their questions.

It made sense to me to present the material in question and answer format since every seller starts the process by asking questions, which will vary depending on whether you're thinking about selling your practice in two to five years or know you've just finished your last tax season. Therefore, start reading with an understanding of where you're at in the process. I recommend that you scan the table of contents; it is organized in an easy to follow format that allows you to quickly select the topics that interest you the most.

I guarantee you'll find answers to questions you didn't know to ask. This book will ensure that you are asking the questions you *should* be asking when you're thinking about selling a tax and accounting practice.

Enjoy and feel free to send me your questions and comments.

Roy Braatz
roy@questbrokers.com

ACKNOWLEDGMENTS

This book would not be possible without the many practice owners who have trusted me with one of their most valuable assets, and the buyers of those practices who took an entrepreneurial leap of faith. I especially want to thank those who trusted my skills early in my career and had faith in me even when my experience did not warrant it. Your encouragement has made this book possible.

I am thankful to Howard Holmes, founder of Accounting Practice Sales, who took a young, energetic guy under his wing and trusted him with the most valuable territory in the company. It has been a pleasure watching APS grow and prosper in this select and specialized area of business sales.

A special thanks goes to the people I've worked with over the years: To Matthew Christie for his many years of professionalism while working with buyers to secure the financing needed to purchase a practice. To Doug Rietz for his expertise in graphic arts; he was instrumental in the design of this book, including its cover and layout. To my attorney, Brian Watkins, for his quality legal advice and common sense approach that's so hard to find in an attorney today. To Bobbie Glover who will turn 70-years-young soon and is still the master communicator—thank you for talking with all those accountants every day! And last but not least, to Jake Hodgkin, who is an expert in so many areas, for his aptitude, character, and ability to work through difficult situations and find acceptable solutions. Jake, you should write a handbook for *buyers* of tax and accounting practices!

ABOUT THE AUTHOR

Roy Braatz has more than 15 years experience in the field of mergers and acquisitions and has operated three successful companies of his own. He currently manages the sale of tax and accounting practices for Accounting Practice Sales in California and serves on the board of directors for Quest Business Brokers, Inc. APS sells more than 250 practices a year. Roy can be reached at *roy@questbrokers.com.*

WHAT IS MY PRACTICE WORTH?

What is My Practice Worth?

The market currently demands a rate of 1.1 to 1.3 times gross revenue. The all-time record approaches 1.4 times gross and some sell at less than 1 times, but these are the extremes. While every seller asks this question, it's also one of the more difficult to answer for any particular practice. In a very real sense every practice sells for the same price: the amount of money a qualified buyer is willing to pay! Also of utmost importance is to remember that price cannot be separated from terms, as will be discussed in the next few chapters. As the saying goes, "You name the price; I'll name the terms."

It is possible for sellers to receive all cash at close and *not guarantee client retention.* Due to years of brainwashing about guaranteeing client retention, this sentence should be read over and over again until it sinks in. To better understand how one receives all cash without guaranteeing client retention, one needs to recognize who the actual buyers are. (See *"Who are the buyers?"*) Also, knowing what is most valuable to buyers in the market is imperative. Ultimately, the open market (your peers) will decide the value of your practice based on what they are willing to pay and how they are willing to pay for it.

Following are the seven factors that have the greatest affect on value.

Recurrence of Revenues: Professional practices generally consist of recurring revenue or a client stream which returns annually for another "drink at the trough." If this important component even appears to be absent, the selling price is affected negatively. For instance, a firm drawing significant income from non-recurring items like litigation support might not be worth as much as one composed largely of traditional tax and write-up. A practice which relies on periodic tax consulting, as opposed to one heavy into on-going tax compliance, will generally be less appealing to prospective buyers.

Size: The size impacts the number of potential buyers. For example, there are many more buyers willing and able to buy a practice with $300,000 of annual gross revenues than one bringing in $2,000,000. A larger pool of potential buyers results in a better multiple. On the other hand, a very small practice might lose value if it is not large enough to support the buyer.

Location: Location also has a great impact on the potential number of buyers and, consequently, on the value. A firm in a metropolitan area often sells for more than one located in the country or a smaller city. In addition, the location within a city itself is important. Much like real estate, a practice in a popular, growing area of a city might receive 10-20% more than an identical practice a few miles down the freeway.

Profitability: Certainly, the greater the net cash flow, the greater the price. Firms with high billing rates and fees are attractive to buyers since this usually translates into less work for more money. However, cash flow is not the dominating determinant that one might presume it would be. Looking at two practices with the same gross revenue, the one with twice the cash flow will not sell for twice the price. Accounting and tax practices are still sold based on gross revenues.

Terms: Price and terms cannot be separated. For example, one buyer may offer $400,000 cash at closing; a second offer could be comprised of a fixed price of $400,000 with $100,000 down and the balance paid with interest over the next two years; still a third buyer may agree to pay $400,000 with 20% down and 20% of collections each year for four years. On the surface these offers may appear to represent the same value, but I assure you they are far from equal. (See next question *"What are the various terms of a sale?"*)

Negative Factors: There are a number of negative variables which impact price. These include anything that affect the buyer's perception of how many clients will eventually be retained and how the purchase will benefit the buyer. Among the many possible problems which may be encountered, some common issues are declining growth, incomplete or missing records, concentration issues (a significant percentage of gross revenue being tied to one or two very large clients), long-term leases, unreasonable transition expectations, or key employees who have not signed a covenant not to compete. Additional problems may also arise when only a portion of a practice is being sold, or a seller plans to continue working in the office after the close of the sale.

Professional Marketing: Every buyer in town loves to see 'FOR SALE BY OWNER' and views it as an opportunity to pay cents on the dollar. A good broker, however, provides essential experience in marketing, negotiation, valuation and financing. More importantly, a specialized broker has access to thousands of buyers immediately. Using a professional almost always results in better prices, better terms, and better buyers.

Price can be laid out on a continuum: On one end we find terms of 20% per year for five years based entirely on collections, and on the other end we find all cash at close. A transaction which involves seller financing but no client retention guarantee is a little to the left of an "all cash at close" deal. To the right of the 20% agreement is the cash deal with a 12 month look back period. In the middle we find the disguised contingency, which appears to be a fixed price but is contingent because the seller has financed the deal and the buyer is totally dependent on the practice to make the payments. Here's where we must discuss the difference between strong and weak buyers—those who allow the seller to lien the equity in their home and those who have no assets to use as collateral.

There remains a misconception that tax and accounting practices have some intrinsic "value" which all potential buyers recognize and with which all agree. If one is selling a gallon of milk this might be true. But people that drink milk purchase it regularly and have a good idea of what it costs. This is not true of tax and accounting practices. Many people in the world would not purchase a practice even if it were offered to them for a dollar. In a metropolitan area of millions, there might only be a couple of hundred potential buyers for a particular practice, in other locations there might be considerably less.

Suppose there are one hundred potential buyers for a specific practice. Would all these buyers agree as to what it was worth? Of course not! They would not even come close to agreement. If a practice is offered at a reduced price, all potential buyers might step up to the plate with check in hand. On the other hand, it could be priced where only one or two would agree to purchase. This is because each buyer has a unique concept as to value, and possesses different degrees of motivation and interest. Sometimes a seller turns away a very motivated and capable buyer because, for one reason or another, the seller decides the buyer is not quite perfect. The seller's misconception is that there are a large number of buyers and that all buyers are equally motivated and equally willing to pay some known price. That misconception could be costly. It is important to be familiar with the market in your geographical area.

This same misconception comes into play when sellers think the only trick is finding "a" buyer. Practice owners routinely say, "Oh, I have a buyer" or "I have someone interested in buying my practice." The implication is that finding a buyer is the hard part. Their assumption, again, is that all buyers are fully willing to pay the same price and terms. While it's possible that "a" buyer is the one willing to pay the best price and terms, it's highly improbable. It's just as likely he is the one willing to pay the least. The object in selling a practice (unlike selling milk) is to first locate all potential buyers for the practice, then from that group determine the top five or ten percent in terms of motivation and ability. It is from this group one must find "the" buyer if one is interested in receiving the true value of the firm.

WHAT ARE THE VARIOUS TERMS OF A SALE?

WHAT ARE THE VARIOUS TERMS OF A SALE?

When a home goes on the market, the seller typically receives the entire payment in cash when the sale is final. The buyer never assumes the seller is willing to finance the transaction. In the sale of CPA or EA firms, the situation is often opposite! Practices have historically sold with seller financing and usually included some type of variable price. Many accounting and tax professionals feel there is no other way to buy or sell, but the fact is there are many other ways to structure the sale of a practice. Understanding today's marketplace will help both buyers and sellers reach mutually beneficial terms.

There are four basic ways firms are sold; two of them involving an adjustable price, and the others maintaining a fixed price.

Seller Guarantee/Adjustable Price

Percentage of Collections: When the seller receives payments based on collections or billings over a period of time, this is referred to as a "percentage of collections" or "percentage of billings". The down payment, percentages, and payout terms vary widely. Traditionally, however, the buyer would pay a down payment of 20% of the estimated price and then pay 20% of collections each year for the first 4 years. This particular scenario is so common that many accountants think it is the *only* way practices can be sold! Understandably, buyers like these terms because payments are manageable and almost all the risk of client retention is transferred to the seller. Buyers will explain there is an "up side" to the seller if the gross revenue increases year after year. However, most sellers are not comfortable assuming retention risk while they have little control over the clients' experience with the new owner. Sellers also dislike the accounting and due diligence involved in calculating the collections year after year. If such a method is used, both the buyer and seller need to be sure everything is spelled out clearly from the beginning, addressing such issues as whether new clients or referrals will be included in the collections, and how "collections" will be applied and accounted for. (See next question *"One times gross—isn't that the law?"*)

Look-back: In this type of sale the buyer "looks back" after a period of time and determines collections or billings; the sales price is then adjusted accordingly. As an example, let's say a buyer agrees to pay $330,000 for a practice that grossed $300,000 the year before the transaction, with a price adjustment of one dollar for each dollar variation in actual collections during the look-back period. In this case, if the practice only ends up collecting $250,000 for year one, the final price would only be $280,000; on the other hand, if the practice collects $330,000, the final price would become $360,000. There are many variations to this method. Although dollar for dollar adjustments are common, there can be alternative price adjustments such as allotting 50 cents for each dollar increased or decreased; or perhaps adjustments may be applied only after a 10% decrease or increase in actual collections; upward and downward caps may be placed on the adjustment, and so on. As you can see, there is room for creativity. This structure is similar to the first method in that the seller guarantees the revenue, but the seller's risk is limited to a shorter period of time. The look-back method does not require seller financing. The seller could receive all cash at close, but then be obligated to refund a portion of the sales price if there is a negative adjustment at the end of the look-back period. In a twelve month look-back, the seller guarantees each client will show up at least once. In the collections scenario, the seller must rely on the buyer's ability to keep the clients coming year after year. The look-back approach is a step closer to a fixed price since the seller has more control; however, the variations can be complicated, making it necessary for each party to be especially certain they understand the implications of each arrangement.

No Guarantee/Fixed Price

Cash: This is when the seller receives 100% of the sales price in cash at closing. The buyer may be obtaining cash from personal funds or, more likely, from a third party lender. Third party financing can actually be more attractive to many buyers, as the payout terms are often extended over ten years rather than the 3-5 years we see when sellers finance the sale; and since most sellers prefer cash at close, this option is a win-win. The cash method has become more and more common in situations where healthy firms in desirable geographic locations change hands. An increase in institutional money available for accounting practice acquisitions, and a marketplace flush with buyers due to broker marketing, have both contributed to the increase in cash sales.

Fixed Price/Seller Financed: In this final method, the sales price is determined prior to close with the seller carrying a portion of the sales price and the price remaining static throughout the life of the loan. When a buyer verbally communicates their intent to make this type of an offer it is important to make sure the buyer is actually considering a fixed price. In view of the fact that traditional deals involve seller financing and an adjustable price based on collections (as described above), a seller may offer to finance a portion of the sales price and the buyer may interpret that to mean they are willing to be paid based on collections.

Seller financing is appealing to buyers for a number of reasons:

1. It is much easier than the bank application and underwriting process.
2. It keeps the seller "in the game" and motivates them to put forth more effort in the transition process (or so the buyer believes).
3. It often comes with more favorable interest rates.

Sellers are more attracted to fixed financing than to guarantee options, but they will still be concerned about collecting full payment. Sufficient down payments, good credit, excellent experience, and proper credentials will be required of the buyer.

Accounting and tax practices are sold today in each of these four ways. As you can see, the premium offered to the seller lies within the deal terms themselves. When a firm is located in a desirable area and the cash flow is strong, it attracts many buyers and ultimately better offers. This usually results in more favorable options for the seller. Conversely, if a practice cannot attract many buyers, terms will favor the buyer. Buyers need to understand the dynamics of each opportunity in order to make the deal work for them. Sellers need to present their practice in a way which attracts the largest number of quality buyers, and since the number of buyers affects the type of deal structure, *using an experienced broker is the way to get the best price and terms!*

ONE TIMES GROSS—
ISN'T THAT THE LAW?

ONE TIMES GROSS—ISN'T THAT THE LAW?

"Accounting practices are worth one times annual gross revenue." This is a belief that has been around the profession for decades and, in fact, still drives the marketplace. No one can really explain why "one times gross" is such an accepted formula, but the most probable theory is that it assumes a backdoor cash flow. Buyers believe they can achieve a certain income level despite what the previous owner has done. Whatever the reason for the widespread thought, it is so persistent that many accountants consider it as some immutable law. They routinely talk of anything above a one times gross as a premium, and anything less as a discount! I have accepted this mindset, using it to my advantage when possible and otherwise working to overcome it.

This ubiquitous mantra implies that accountants value practices with reference to annual gross revenues. This is unique to accounting and tax practices. Almost all other small businesses are valued based on a multiple of *net cash flow* to the owner (including salary, payroll taxes, benefits, profits, etc.), which is commonly called discretionary cash flow. For small businesses in North America that multiple is about 2.4 times cash flow to owner. The multiple for service businesses is less, more like 1.5 to 2 times; therefore, if accountants were like everyone else, they would value their businesses at 1.5 to 2 times this discretionary cash flow. But they are different. Sometimes, where the cash flow is high, the "1 times gross" mindset hurts the value of a practice; at other times, when cash flow is low, it helps the value.

Be aware that, despite common beliefs, not all practices sell at one times gross. This would be like saying houses sell for $X a square foot. Some do and some don't. There are a whole host of factors that will make a practice sell for more or less than another practice. They include location, cash flow, type, size, etc.

One times gross is the starting point because that is the common conception of the masses, but it is probably better to think in terms of a range like 80-120% of gross as being more realistic. Sellers and buyers need to move out of the mindset that every practice is the same and is valued the same; surely no one believes that each accounting or tax firm is a "cookie cutter" image of the one down the street. Knowledge of what makes one practice more attractive than another is a major reason sellers and buyers should consider using an experienced broker who specializes in tax and accounting practices.

Everyone's definition of the multiple of gross differs. Deals have failed at the signing table when the buyer and seller realized they were talking apples and oranges. It is imperative that terms are understood and distinctions clearly stated early in the process.

In these discussions, it is also necessary to decide what is included in the calculation of gross revenue. First of all, what is being considered—billings or collections? It is a given that accountants should understand the difference in accrual and cash basis accounting better than anyone, but when it comes to buying or selling a practice these differences are often ignored. Cash basis is often used but accrual can sometimes be a better indicator. At any rate, buyer and seller need to understand what is being presented. Second of all, what period of time is considered in the calculation? There certainly does not seem to be a standard consensus. Is the last calendar year the determinant? Or do the parties use the most recent 12 month period? Does one look at an average of the last three years or so? Or does the year after the sale become the period under consideration? All of those measurements are used by one party or the other and often without prior discussion. That can lead to problems. One can not begin to discuss 100% of gross as a value without knowing what gross is. To peg value at a multiple of gross, it is necessary to know what exactly is considered as a part of the sale. Are furniture and equipment included or are these added to the "one times gross"? What about accounts receivable, accounts payable or work in process? Obviously, there are many factors to consider.

The assets sold in the sale of an accounting practice are those necessary for the new owner to continue operating the business. Generally, this includes client files, client lists, non-compete agreements and property assets like furniture, equipment and software. The truth of the matter is that used furniture and equipment are not considered to have much value; in fact, some buyers do not even want them. They rarely affect the overall value. Usually the seller retains cash and accounts receivable, while work in process is often lumped into the sales price or possibly prorated. The seller is generally responsible for all existing debt at the time of the sell. Leases should also be discussed up front.

While one times gross is not a law, it is still very prevalent in the thinking of both sellers and buyers and cannot be dismissed. It is a general guideline and nothing more. It is best to realize, however, that prices do vary up and down from this simplistic "standard." It is also best to remember some simple rules of economics. 1) Value is set by the buyer; sellers and brokers can determine an asking price but not the final value. If there are *no* buyers the practice is worth nothing. 2) In an efficient market, quality will command a higher price. Lackluster practices are hard to sell no matter what the gross. 3) The larger the pool of buyers, the greater the demand and, consequently, the greater the value. Buyers and sellers will most likely get the best and fairest deals if they consider these principles.

WHO BEARS THE RISK OF CLIENT RETENTION?

WHO BEARS THE RISK OF CLIENT RETENTION?

When all is said and done, the key to success in the accounting and tax profession is retention of paying clients. All practices must be able to retain clients in order to survive and thrive. We know that. We also know there is no absolute guarantee clients will stay, whether the current owner is in place or a new buyer. No one owns the clients and no one can force them to stay. *In theory, every single client could leave tomorrow!* Yet we don't worry too much about this because clients can and have been retained successfully for years and even decades. All the studies show, and experience confirms, the majority of clients return when we treat them right, solve their problems, and simply meet their needs.

So why is there such a fear of client attrition once a practice changes ownership? Why is client retention the number one concern of all buyers and most sellers? There is the wide-spread perception that a "bond" exists between clients and professionals that will be broken in a sale and may be difficult to reestablish between clients and the new owner. An over-exaggerated assumption exists which states the change of ownership *itself* will cause clients to leave the firm for a competitor or they will start doing the work themselves. Occasionally, this concern is validated by the horror stories of some poor buyer who purchased a practice and lost two-thirds of the clients. *However, the truth is that under circumstances involving an average amount of care and common sense, client retention rates for a new owner are often in line with the retention rates experienced by the previous owner and perhaps even greater!*

Let's take a look at the client's perspective. The client may be disappointed about the change. There was a relationship of trust in place, and no one likes to see a trusted advisor retire. In addition to this issue, most people just do not like change. However, these issues are easy enough for a buyer to overcome.

Sure, the client loved working with the former owner and is stunned to think life must go on without this trusted advisor and friend. But once the initial shock is out of the way, what are the client's options? The client still needs accounting and tax services and still needs an accountant. Those who have planned ahead may have an alternative in their back pocket. Others may have a cousin who, for years, has been trying to convince them they can "do the books cheaper". These cases, however, are rare. For most people the only real option is to go to the Yellow Pages and that, of course, can be a nightmare. Even transferring the records over to the neighbor or cousin is going to be far more inconvenient than checking out the new owner.

The best option for the client is almost always to give the new owner a try. After all, the new owner already has the files and can be found at the same phone number and often the same address as the previous owner. Usually the same employees are there and hopefully the prices are about the same. The client usually assumes, and will be informed via an introduction letter, that the professional they have trusted for years has "hand picked" the new owner. What this comes down to is convenience; convenience is often a top priority for the client. Searching for a new accountant and conducting multiple interviews can be a very exhausting and time-consuming venture. Staying with the new owner is the path of least resistance, and the client should have a certain level of comfort based on the previous owner's recommendation, especially if the buyer reaches out immediately once the sale is final.

"But how can I make sure the clients will stay with me?" the buyer asks. The answer is simple: An accountant retains new clients the same way he or she retains any client. Again, if a buyer treats clients with respect and professionalism, and meets their needs, the client will stay and pay. A 100% retention rate is unreasonable—we realize that—some clients may be lost just because the change gives them a chance to go to that neighbor or cousin, or to find someone closer.

However, the number of people who jump ship due to a change in ownership is not nearly as high as most believe.

Who has control over retention? The buyer, the seller, and the clients themselves each carry a role in ensuring a continuous relationship. After the seller has sent out an introduction letter, performed key introductions, and completed the transition, it is the buyer who makes decisions regarding quality of service, pricing, and anything else affecting client satisfaction. Typically, the seller will be available to assist the buyer with endorsement letters, occasional problem solving and words of encouragement. However, the seller's ultimate contribution to the deal is to bring the goodwill of the clients to the closing table, provide a list of persons with the need for accounting services, and use his or her influence to encourage clients to give the new owner a try. The seller simply owes the buyer his good faith and support during transition. In short, although the seller assists in retaining clients, the bulk of the control, by far, is with the buyer. If the new owner does not treat the clients well and provide fair solutions, they will leave no matter what the seller says or does. (See *"What is the best way to transition clients?"*)

What are the Risks of Buying a Practice?

What Are the Risks of Buying a Practice?

Sellers have virtually no control over the success or failure of the practice after close. The seller's job is to recommend the buyer to the clients, and then to stop servicing them and get out of the way. The buyer's job is to provide quality service. The buyer's attitude will determine client retention and overall success.

This does not mean the transaction is risk-free. The three risks in a practice transition are 1) employees, 2) large clients and 3) buyer apathy. If the buyer focuses on these key elements, they will be 90% of the way to success in a new practice.

Employees: It is my experience that buyers and sellers worry too much about clients in the transition process and too little about employees. They are anxious that clients "do not like change," or are overly concerned with what will happen to the "long-term relationship", whether clients will go somewhere else. All of that worry is overblown. Clients do not want change, but they have no choice. If the seller refuses to do their work any longer, they will change accountants. The only question is, "To whom?" If the buyer has their file, the seller's recommendation, and is the first one to talk with them about their needs, virtually all of the clients will give the buyer a chance. Client transition is not a big problem. That is, unless an employee sets up shop down the street and solicits the client's business.

Case: Two weeks before closing the sale of an accounting practice, a long-time employee of the practice, a bookkeeper who had just taken his CPA exam, quits. Virtually all of the bookkeeping clients they worked with, and a good number of tax returns, went with him. **Case:** A buyer purchases a practice grossing $210,000. The only employees were the seller and a seven year CPA. The long-term employee had left earlier in the year (before the buyer presented an offer) to go to work with her husband in his CPA firm. The buyer does not see this as a major problem because the seller says, "Since she is having a baby, she and her husband will be too busy to take on more work." A year after closing, the practice gross is down 20%. **Case:** A seller puts his practice on the market because his long-term CPA, whom he had been grooming to buy the practice, leaves to go work for someone else. His ex-employee takes some clients, but by closing, it has been almost a year and he "hasn't lost any more clients in the last couple of months." The buyer's gross is down 30% in year one after the former employee sends letters out to all of the practice's clients following the sale.

Most employees are not currently conspiring to take all of the business. It's rare that an employee has the entrepreneurial bug at all, but for those that do, it can become an overwhelming temptation. Sellers should consider employee risk and if risks are identified then maybe non-competition or client purchase agreements are in order. A modest payment could accompany this request and smooth the way. A competent attorney should be retained to draft these agreements.

Large clients: Virtually all clients will give the buyer a chance. However, a real risk occurs when the practice has one client representing an unusually large percentage of the gross billings. Purchasing a practice with 300 clients and retaining 299 of them would be a great success, unless the one you lost represents 25% of the gross revenue for the practice. Sellers would be wise to ask themselves such questions as: Does any one client represent 10% or more of the gross revenue? What are the revenues of the top ten producing clients? Are any so large as to represent a significant problem? Is there any indication these clients are selling their business or otherwise going away?

Most clients represent such a small part of the practice, a buyer can lose one to two percent in transition and not feel it. Buyers and sellers should pay attention to the big ones. While practices with revenue concentration can be a wonderful opportunity, they must be handled properly.

Buyer apathy: Most successful practices are "marketing oriented." I'm not referring to marketing for new clients but rather *marketing to current clients.* Successful accountants constantly sell themselves to their current clients. Any interaction with a client is judged in terms of the impression that it leaves on the client. Are we increasing the client's confidence in us? Are we building the client's confidence that we are giving them good service and that we are attentive to their needs? Do we make them feel that we are competent and that they are being cared for?

In the area of client transition, it is especially important that buyers take an active, marketing approach. Buyers should budget a lot of time to sell themselves to the clients. This is not the seller's time; it is the *buyer's* time. They need to go see the large clients. They need to take them to lunch. They need to impress new clients with their level of service and concern, and understanding of their needs. When purchasing a list of tax clients, buyers can not be content with sending a letter and then burying their heads in the sand. Their job is not waiting for the clients to come in and then prepare their taxes accurately and correctly. Instead, they should bury themselves in the task of marketing to the clients. Call them up before the end of the year. Talk to them about their tax situation; see if there is anything that can be done to help them before the year's end. Tell them about the new tax law. Talk to them about how they would like to bring in their return information. Suggest that they allow extra time this year to visit so that the buyer can get to know them. The danger of buyer apathy is further enhanced by a misunderstanding of the seller's role in transition. Many buyers and sellers think that the seller needs to help in the transition by being around for months, or even years. This is a mistake and shows a lack of understanding of the process of transition. When the seller is around, the danger is it will lead to the buyer being less intense about their need to sell themselves to the clients. I've sold practices in early February to buyers that already own a practice. You can imagine how much time they had during tax season to market themselves to the new clients—they had none. Some worked out an agreement with the seller to continue through tax season and perform most of the service for the clients. The buyers bury themselves in their former client's needs and do little to sell themselves to the new clients. However, these clients cannot be ignored forever. In doing this, the buyers set themselves up for substantial losses.

When purchasing a practice, it is very important that buyers realize the need to spend a considerable amount of time getting to know the new clients and marketing themselves to them. Buyers who do this will successfully sell themselves to ninety-nine percent of clients. Those who fail to do so are putting their investment at great risk.

How Long Will it Take to Sell My Practice?

HOW LONG WILL IT TAKE TO SELL MY PRACTICE?

Any answer to this question is only a guess. On average, the turnaround time from start to finish is 3-6 months. Obviously, the time of year makes a difference. Even so, there's never a bad time to begin marketing a practice—marketing through tax season often skews the average but can also create a pool of potential buyers who are ready to move forward in May.

There are so many variables which impact timing that it is impossible to cover them all here, but a few of them are: 1) Pure tax practices sell much faster toward the end of the calendar year, cash flow being the main factor. 2) Practices in a "Hot Market" with a dense population will sell, on average, faster than practices in rural areas because of the number of potential buyers. 3) Size—There are many more buyers for a $300,000 practice than a $1,000,000 practice. The number of potential buyers is dramatically decreased when the purchase price is substantially increased.

We have found "bargain basement" pricing is ineffective and in fact deters buyers when the practice is professionally marketed. Sophisticated buyers see red flags when a practice is priced below market. What a seller may feel is a reason to set a low asking price, the buyer may feel is a reason to bid up the practice. This works in reverse as well. The key to attracting buyers quickly is to disclose as many details about the practice as possible while maintaining confidentiality. (See "*What should be provided to the buyer prior to the first meeting?*")

In summary, the time of year, market conditions, and the type, size, location and price of a practice will influence the length of a sale. Regardless, the best time to get started is when the owner is ready to sell.

WHAT IS THE BEST WAY TO TRANSITION CLIENTS?

What is the Best Way to Transition Clients?

Transition is most effective when approached on an individual client basis. Think like a client and decide what would motivate you to give a new practitioner a shot at your business, then proceed accordingly.

Every client should receive an introduction letter from the seller and a letter plus phone call from the buyer introducing himself. The buyer must be proactive in contacting clients; writing letters, making phone calls, stopping by at their business, inviting higher level clients to lunch—whatever it takes. The seller knows these clients and should give advice concerning each of them. Compensation for the introduction and for transition advice is usually included in the purchase price of the practice.

Let's apply this situation to an area which is sensitive to all of us—our teeth! Think about what you'd want as a patient if your dentist sold his practice. If you merely received a letter from the new practitioner and nothing else—would you consider going to another dentist the next time your tooth ached? What if you received a letter, followed later by a quick one-minute phone call from the new dentist, introducing himself and expressing his excitement over caring for your dental health? What if the call was two minutes and he told you about his schooling and expertise in the field? How would you feel about a free checkup—no strings attached—because he'd really like to meet you and become familiar with your teeth so that he can better serve your needs? Now, when the pain comes, will you be going to the new replacement your previous dentist recommended, where your charts and x-rays reside, or will you be hitting Google in an attempt to find a new dentist?

A qualified buyer of an accounting practice will not have a problem understanding the technical aspect of a client file, but what he won't have is a historical perspective. The most effective thing a seller can do to help in this regard is to write a quick note in each client's file—it can be a small post-it—and give some tidbit about that client. Again, imagine going into that new dentist, sitting down, and having him say "Nice to meet you. How's that shoulder been feeling since your surgery last year?" or "How's your daughter Beth doing in college?" If the buyer can point to a personal item of interest that doesn't involve their finances, he'll have a client for life. It shows that his previous practitioner cared enough to mention him individually to the buyer and the buyer cared enough to listen.

In retaining clients, there is no magic formula, but here are some ideas to consider:

- Send a personal holiday greeting.
- Host a meet and greet at the office for select clients, or all clients, if possible. Include the staff so that clients recognize familiar faces.
- Follow the seller's previous protocol for sending organizers or appointment reminder cards.
- Offer a free half hour tax planning session between the time of purchase and the year's end, just to meet and warm up those clients before tax season. This not only helps retain the clients but could also result in providing additional services.
- Remember you never get a second chance to make a good first impression.

While transitioning clients, the buyer should never underestimate the power of the employees and their influence. Care must be taken in order to demonstrate that the buyer understands their value and importance, using any means necessary to ensure the loyalty of their new employees; encouraging communication, expressing words of gratitude, and perhaps even taking the staff out for a night on the town.

A word of caution: Beware of encouraging sellers to stick around for the first tax season! Introducing clients in person or continuing to work with them actually prevents successful transitioning and creates confusion! The clients are not bonding with the buyer when the seller is in the room. Regardless of the size of practice, one of the best things a seller can do for the buyer is to spend 4-6 weeks accomplishing a few of the ideas discussed and then to disappear (from the office, anyway). We've seen buyers fool themselves by insisting on a 12 month revenue guarantee and asking the seller to stay during the first tax season. They hit their revenue numbers in year one, pay the seller the asking price, and then, thinking transition is complete, neglect to form their own relationships, which results in a loss of clients.

Remember that in business there's such a thing as an invaluable person, but no such thing as an indispensable one.

What is the Law Regarding the Transfer of Client Files?

WHAT IS THE LAW REGARDING THE TRANSFER OF CLIENT FILES?

I wish someone could answer this question with authority, but there doesn't appear to be enough legal precedence available, and the written law is somewhat fuzzy. Below is an opinion from a seller's attorney who was involved in a transaction I brokered in California—take it for what it's worth:

Re: Client confidentiality in the context of the sale of an accounting practice.

Roy Braatz has brought up the issue of client confidentiality in connection with the proposed sale of Mr. X's practice. Because the sale will of necessity involve review of and the receipt of confidential accounting client files by the buyer, the question arises: Must Mr. X obtain written consent from each client before selling his practice and transferring the files?

Based on the California Business & Professions Code, as well as the AICPA rules, I conclude the answer is firmly no. The parties may go through with the sale, and the resulting files transfer, without the written consent of Mr. X's current clients.

As a starting point of the analysis, California Business & Professions Code § 5063.3 provides:

> *(a) No confidential information obtained by a licensee, in his or her professional capacity, concerning a client or a prospective client shall be disclosed by the licensee without the written permission of the client or prospective client, except the following: (4) Disclosures made by a licensee or a licensee's duly authorized representative to another licensee in connection with a proposed sale or merger of the licensee's professional practice.*

While the above analytical text does not include such words as "accounting" or "accountant", B&P § 5063.3 is within the Chapter for Accountants and Accounting practices. Also, regarding the above code section, I found nothing restricting or qualifying the exemption provided for the sale/purchase of an accounting practice.

Turning to the AICPA, the relevant rules provide:

> *Rule 301 – Confidential client information. A member in public practice shall not disclose any confidential client information without the specific consent of the client.*
>
> *Rule 301.3 – Confidential information and the purchase, sale, or merger of a practice. Rule 301 [ET section 301.01] prohibits a member in public practice from disclosing any confidential client information without the specific consent of the client. The rule provides that it shall not be construed to prohibit the review of a member's professional practice under AICPA or state CPA society authorization.*
>
> *For purposes of rule 301 [ET section 301.01], a review of a member's professional practice is hereby authorized to include a review in conjunction with a prospective purchase, sale, or merger of all or part of a member's practice. The member must take appropriate precautions (for example, through a written confidentiality agreement) so that the prospective purchaser does not disclose any information obtained in the course of the review, since such information is deemed to be confidential client information.*
>
> *Members reviewing a practice in connection with a prospective purchase or merger shall not use to their advantage nor disclose any member's confidential client information that comes to their attention.*

Translation: Rule 301.3 provides an exemption to Rule 301 in the case of the sale/purchase of an entire practice, provided that "appropriate precautions" are taken. Rule 301.3, in its own text, provides a written confidentiality agreement as an example of an "appropriate precaution".

Another concern is the last paragraph which provides a "prospective purchase[r] . . . shall not use to their advantage . . . " any confidential information. While the rule does not define this, and I am not aware of any more precise definition within the California Business & Professions Code, some states provide examples which imply that upon the sale, the purchaser *may not* sell any one or any subset of the files to some other accounting practice *without first obtaining written consent from the clients.*

Taking all of this into consideration, it is my conclusion that no need exists to obtain written consent from each client for the transfer of Mr. X's current files, provided that: 1) The buyer executes a confidentiality agreement regarding the client files, 2) The buyer uses the information only for the purpose of the continued provision of accounting services to the clients, and for no other purpose, and 3) The buyer refrains from selling and/or referring any of Mr. X's clients, unless it is in the context of selling the entire practice some time in the future.

CAN I SELL MY PRACTICE AND RETAIN A NUMBER OF CLIENTS?

CAN I SELL MY PRACTICE AND RETAIN A NUMBER OF CLIENTS?

Yes. This happens quite often, but it is important to consider the buyer's possible objections. If the buyer feels that the seller is "cherry picking" the good clients and selling the balance, it is difficult to attract a strong offer.

Following are a few exceptions which are acceptable to buyers:

- The seller may desire to retain all mail-in clients—those that have moved out of the area over the years and continue to mail everything in. (Clients within the vicinity would be included in the sale, even if their work is done by mail.) Cash buyers don't object to this because those clients tend to be a higher flight risk, making them less desirable revenue in an all cash transaction.

- The seller may choose to retain one or two close friends and relatives. This is pretty self-explanatory; these clients are often serviced at a discount, or even for free, causing the buyer to be more than willing to allow the seller to retain them.

- Occasionally a seller will decide to restructure their practice. They may want to sell all the 1040 work in order to concentrate solely on business clients; or perhaps they would like to let go of all audit work in order to exit that arena; any such combinations are reasonable as long as they don't involve capturing the profitable clients and leaving the undesirable remains to the buyer.

- Often the seller holds on to one or two very large clients and sells the balance of the practice. Much like the mail-in clients, larger accounts present a higher risk to the buyer, especially when the client consists of 10% or more of the gross revenue.

There may be many reasons a seller desires to retain clients, but if they expect a quality offer then the buyer must feel that the book of business being sold is appropriately valued.

Will I Be Required to Sign a Non-Compete?

WILL I BE REQUIRED TO SIGN A NON-COMPETE?

To put it simply, yes. No buyer in his right mind is going to purchase a practice while leaving the seller with the option of setting up shop down the street once they decide retirement isn't all it's made up to be. That being said, let's explore the two most common types of non-compete arrangements:

- The first arrangement simply applies to the clients being sold. It goes on to say the seller will not give any other person or firm the right to solicit those same clients. When the seller is obviously retirement age, is selling his entire practice without retaining any clients and is showing no interest in continuing to work in public accounting, this satisfies most buyers.

- The second most common provision involves listing the terms above, but adding a specified geographical area. This range can be from 5 miles in densely populated areas to 50 miles, or even an entire state, depending on the seller's type of practice and reach. A seller who is not yet retirement age and is willing to continue in public accounting will probably be signing some sort of geographical non-compete. A seller that retains all mail-in clients could sign a geographical non-compete within a 5 mile radius and be free to service those long-distance clients. The buyer simply doesn't want the seller opening an office nearby and becoming his competition.

When a buyer uses bank financing in order to pay the seller cash at close, a bank underwriter will often require a geographical non-compete as part of the bank's due diligence review of the purchase agreement.

As you can see, the first arrangement leaves flexibility for the seller to continue in the accounting profession while the second can eliminate this ability to a larger degree. Both non-competes are simple to understand, are only one paragraph long, and are incorporated into the purchase contract. Occasionally the buyer's attorney will come up with a 10-page non-compete that takes a law degree to decipher, but this is rare and unrealistic.

Should I Sell and Transition Over a Number of Years?

SHOULD I SELL AND TRANSITION OVER A NUMBER OF YEARS?

This question is asked either by those who mistakenly assume a long transition is required (See *"What is the best way to transition clients?"*), or by owners who aren't quite ready to retire, but no longer want to deal with the day-to-day responsibilities of running the business.

There are several items that should be seriously considered before selling a practice and continuing to work for the buyer:

- The buyer simply cannot afford to retain the seller as an employee after paying a fair market price for the practice. Whether the buyer pays cash and has a third party debt service, or the deal is contingent and the buyer owes the seller a percentage of billables; the cost of paying the seller a market salary, handling the debt service, *and* generating cash for the buyer's living expenses is too great.

- The seller is much better off keeping the practice, pocketing the entire net income for the next 3-5 years and then selling it for whatever the market will bear. Of course, if the seller is insistent on getting out of management, a sale is possible; however, the practice would be worth considerably less.

- Sticking around for years has a way of ending badly for the seller. Most practice owners were employees at one time or another and their disdain for employment is why they ventured out as entrepreneurs to manage their own practices. It's hard enough finding good employees, much less finding a good boss—if you've been self-employed for years, you may not appreciate the new environment. Unraveling these transactions is nearly impossible without catastrophic damage to equity.

- It generally creates upheaval in the client base. Client A is assigned to the new guy while you continue to service Client B. When Client A runs into Client B and finds out that you've shuffled him off while retaining Client B—well, you finish the story. Client retention is a bigger concern in these scenarios than it is in an outright purchase where the seller walks away.

The bottom line is, selling a practice and continuing to work for the new owner is a bad idea. Consider some alternate means that may relieve the strain—raise your fees so that a number of clients leave and the workload is reduced; sell off the 1040 work and retain the business clients; buy another practice that includes top notch staff—taking the practice to "the next level"...

WHAT WILL THE BUYER REQUEST TO SEE IN DUE DILIGENCE?

WHAT WILL THE BUYER REQUEST TO SEE IN DUE DILIGENCE?

This varies widely from practice to practice and from buyer to buyer. These transactions involve a high degree of trust; when the buyer trusts the seller, due diligence is usually a simple process which shouldn't take more than a couple of days.

Every transaction calls for due diligence; this protects both the buyer and the seller. For the buyer, due diligence is an opportunity to validate their understanding of the practice using hard data. It is equally advantageous to the seller because once due diligence is complete, there is no room for the buyer to shift blame based on miscommunication or misrepresentation.

It is also important to understand that the timing of due diligence should always be *after* the buyer's offer is accepted. Many buyers feel that full due diligence should be performed prior to making an offer, but the proper method is for the seller to provide enough information up front, enabling the buyer to make a completely educated offer. (See *"Why is there no detailed due diligence prior to my offer?"*)

Below is a reasonable due diligence list a buyer might submit. (Remember, the seller has already provided financial statements from the previous three years, an interim financial statement, a breakdown of service mix showing how revenue was derived, information about the premises lease and expiration and a breakdown of employees and their responsibilities. (See next question *"What should be provided to the buyer prior to the first meeting?"*)

Operations:

1. Review accounts receivable aging. (Even though the buyer won't be purchasing the AR, reviewing the accounts can reveal problematic clients.)

2. Randomly examine client files to confirm the buyer's direct experience with various types of clients and services.

3. Reconcile bank statements to cash receipts reported.

4. Discuss the employees of the firm to anticipate any competitive threat, determine skill levels, and ascertain any future hiring needs. (This does not involve the employees, who are generally unaware of the sale until after the close.)

5. Review current software and systems.

Questions for the Seller:

1. Are there any client groupings that make up a large percentage of revenue?

2. What are the average ages of clients?

3. How often do you meet with clients?

4. When was the last fee increase?

5. Do you send out organizers, and when?

6. Is there any pending litigation?

7. When and how do clients set appointments for tax season?

8. What is the average number of new clients per month?

9. What are the sources of new clients?

10. Is there any leased equipment?

Other items to be reviewed and discussed may surface throughout this procedure. It's quite normal for buyers to find some "red flags"— that's what due diligence is for. Every practice has some weak points. Buyers learn the details and go in with eyes wide open. There is no perfect practice and there is no perfect buyer, but that doesn't mean there can't be a perfect match.

What Should be Provided to the Buyer Prior to the First Meeting?

WHAT SHOULD BE PROVIDED TO THE BUYER PRIOR TO THE FIRST MEETING?

The more detail a seller can provide the buyer prior to meeting, the better. Of course, if the seller is concerned about anonymity, they must not provide information which easily identifies their particular practice in their specific geographical location. This is easier in large metropolitan areas than in small rural areas.

Why is it important to provide details before the meeting? A confidential overview of the opportunity acts as another filter to reduce the number of individuals who are aware the practice is for sale. While still concealing the name of the seller, buyers who prove qualified receive more specific details about the practice. After reviewing the information, they may realize the practice isn't a good fit for them—fees too low for their style, fees too high for their experience level, a real estate lease which is more than they can assume—and they eliminate themselves, reducing the number of buyers a seller must meet with. Thus, prior to meeting, the seller should provide the following:

1. Reason for selling.

2. Brief history of the business (again, without pointing directly at the practice).

3. Strengths and weaknesses of the practice.

4. Software being used.

5. Three years of financials and interim information (these should include add backs to arrive at the total discretionary net income).

6. Asking price and terms.

7. A service mix breakdown, showing how revenue is generated.

8. Description of facilities and real estate lease commitment.

9. Employee summary—their titles, years employed, compensation, billing rate, duties and whether they are degreed or licensed.

Obviously, not all of these items will apply to every practice, but these are the basics. If marketing a highly specialized practice, even in a big city, it may be difficult to give these details without losing anonymity; a seller must simply provide as much information as possible prior to meeting the buyers.

The details provided prior to meeting will help reduce the number of unnecessary buyer meetings, make for a more effective meeting with qualified buyers, and serve as a preview to due diligence in order to help the buyer make the next step: *presenting an offer*. Sellers should not become involved in due diligence before an offer has been accepted (See *"Why is there no detailed due diligence prior to my offer?"* in Questions Buyers Ask); the buyer should have enough information prior to meeting the seller to make an offer!

WHAT TOPICS SHOULD BE AVOIDED IN BUYER MEETINGS?

WHAT TOPICS SHOULD BE AVOIDED IN BUYER MEETINGS?

Neither price nor terms should come up in the initial meeting; a compatibility check is the objective at this stage. Buyers must *want* the practice before they will present an attractive offer; they generally aren't excited until they meet the seller in person and learn more about the practice. This initial meeting is neither the time nor the place to set the stage of negotiations. Oftentimes, buyers will submit a low offer to feel the seller out; in order to get top dollar the seller needs to play the game, and play it right!

If the seller has decided not to utilize a broker, they would do well to take this bit of advice: Have someone acting as a buffer to negotiate the price and terms for you—your trusted attorney, your cousin, your mother, someone! Could you discuss price and terms directly with the buyer and hammer it out? Absolutely; but there's a reason every multi-billion dollar transaction is brokered by an investment banker—the seller puts himself at a distinct disadvantage by negotiating directly with the buyer. Things are said, and taken, out of context; sensitive issues are discussed directly, and people take a defensive position, which never results in a positive outcome. For example, if the seller were to personally present counter offers and ideas, it is possible they may produce a "knee jerk" reaction with the buyer, causing hard feelings between them as a consequence. It would then be very difficult at that point to recover the transaction. However, if the go-between were to present the ideas, the relationship with the buyer would remain healthy, regardless of whether the buyer was unhappy with the negotiations. Sellers are often concerned about addressing sensitive issues. As a broker, it is my job to communicate those issues to the buyer and personally take the heat of the battle. This allows the seller to later explain that the *crazy broker* made them bring up such-and-such a point!

What Other Pitfalls Should I Avoid When Selling?

What Other Pitfalls Should I Avoid When Selling?

Although it may repeat some of the information already provided, presented here is a *laundry list* of dangerous hazards to avoid. My hope is that it will stimulate some thought about other questions pertaining to your unique situation.

Pitfalls to Avoid

Selling with a contingency: The buyer has the primary control over client retention; therefore, the seller generally should not bear this risk. The seller cannot afford to have their retirement rest on what someone else does two or three years from now.

Selling too cheaply: Practice owners who sell on their own often end up selling for a discount, or under inferior terms and conditions. Without a broker, it is difficult to understand the market in the area, especially the quantity and quality of potential buyers.

Carrying a note when unnecessary: Seller financing is not the only option. Financing options are plentiful and there is a good chance a buyer will pay 100% cash at closing. If you have your own buyer, ask a broker for referrals to quality lenders. (See *"What options are available in financing a practice?"*)

Wasting time with unqualified buyers: Don't waste time with buyers who are not serious or do not have the ability to take over your legacy! Have a system for screening a buyer's willingness to pay a fair price, their ability to get financing, and their capacity to make a success out of the acquisition. Be certain every buyer has signed a binding confidentiality agreement prior to notifying them of the sale. (See *"How are buyers pre-qualified?"*)

Attempting to sell to an employee or partner: This would seem to be the ideal scenario but, in reality, it rarely works well for the seller. Finding the right replacement or partner can be disappointing; even in a favorable situation the seller is forced to adapt to the potential buyer's timetable. These arrangements usually lead to long payouts, discounted sales prices, and unwanted contingencies.

Not using a specialized broker: When choosing a broker, certainly don't hire a general business broker, they will not understand how the tax and accounting profession works. The broker should be a specialist in the area of accounting and tax practice acquisitions and should be aware of a seller's most common concerns, including how the seller's reputation, clients, and staff will be affected by the different marketing approaches and negotiation styles. (See *"Why should I hire a broker?"*)

Paying in advance for brokerage services: No broker with solid existing buyers and experience is going to ask for an upfront fee of any kind. Avoid the broker who requires any payment whatsoever before the sale's proceeds reach your bank account.

Waiting too long: You have invested a great deal of time and effort into your business and it has paid off. Why not go ahead and pursue those other dreams while you still have the opportunity to enjoy them? Sell when you are on the top of your game.

What Happens if I Can't Sell my Practice?

WHAT HAPPENS IF I CAN'T SELL MY PRACTICE?

Many practice owners are convinced the sale of their practice will add a nice bonus to their retirement fund, but we all know it's never a good idea to count our chickens before they hatch. Selling a practice is anything but certain. Location, demographics of buyers, and good old competition have a huge influence on the market. It's the combination of many variables that determines market demand and it is market demand that determines whether a practice sells or just sits there.

Those practices grossing more than $2 million and less than $5 million lie in the "no man's land" of practice sales—not large enough to generally attract the big regional firms, and too large for individual buyers or smaller firms in the market. Owners of these practices should contact me on a case-by-case basis for recommendations.

This book is written specifically for practices grossing up to $2 million. There are some circumstances which make these sales more difficult, such as having a rural location, more than one owner, specialized and undesirable niches, and revenue concentration issues. Following are some possible solutions to these various circumstances.

Rural practices: Start training clients to mail everything in—refuse to see anyone in person. You'll lose some clients, but those who remain will be better prepared to go with a buyer that might not be local—someone willing to purchase your practice. Start raising fees to match those charged in larger cities closest to you. Many buyers are turned off by rural practices because their fees are too low.

More than one owner: This is a difficult situation. Single buyers can't replace the current owners and other firms don't have the qualified manpower to take over for multiple partners. Turning a client who is accustomed to dealing with an owner-operator over to a staff person is a formula for disaster, and they know it. The best solution, although not always viable, is for the current owners to split into separate legal entities and have an expense-sharing arrangement for rent and staff; they can then be financed and sold separately to individual buyers. If this is impossible, the partners should take a close look at billable hours and determine if one or maybe two buyers could handle the workload. In some cases, a single buyer may be able to handle the load of two exiting partners who have cut back over the years and have minimal billable hours; or perhaps a husband/wife team buying a practice could manage the work of three partners that are exiting. The only other solutions left are: 1) to sell portions of revenue to willing buyers, which can include one partner's clients or a mix of many partners' clients, or 2) to sell the entire practice to another firm at whatever price the market will bear. This second option may be a fine alternative but be sure not to count your retirement dollars in the process. Right now, some of you are thinking "How about just selling one partner's equity and having a new partner?" This is possible, but involves so much work that it's not worth mentioning the details. The bottom line is, selling firms with multiple partners, especially firms grossing more than $2 million, is very difficult.

Niche practices: If your practice is in Hollywood and every client is a post production sound person, prepare to wait some time for a buyer. Buyers must feel comfortable with the work involved or they generally won't buy. I won't go into great detail here, as there's little you can do to improve the situation; hopefully you're in a big city that has potential buyers for your niche. If there's ever going to be a buyer for the above practice, he or she will reside in Hollywood, Nashville or Manhattan. If all your clients are car dealerships or McDonald's franchisees then the buyer doesn't need specific industry experience as much as confidence working with that caliber of client; the rest can be learned over time. If you are not looking to sell immediately, consider diversifying by bringing in some different types of clients to help alleviate this concentration.

Revenue concentration: If one or two clients represent 10% or more of the revenue then there could be a concentration issue. Not many buyers will pay cash with this sort of risk hanging out there, but there are ways to work around it. Two possible solutions would include: 1) The practice could be priced on a cash basis excluding those concentration clients who are sold on a contingent basis; a two step process that is fair to buyer and seller, or 2) The seller could retain the concentration clients and sell the rest of the practice, assuming the practice is still profitable without those clients. These examples are only two of any number of formulas that could be put into place and assure a fair transaction for both parties while not exposing the seller to the full risk of client retention.

Selling a practice is all about supply and demand. Knowing what type of buyers are active in the market will help position the practice properly for sale. Today's buyer can be young and much more diverse, with a new generation of practitioners who, in many ways, are rewriting the rules.

If you can't sell your practice, you have two or three possible options:

1. Keep running it. This is obvious enough, but consider changing some things to make your life more bearable. I'm not a practice consultant, but raising fees and firing grumpy clients could make ownership more attractive for you and help to eventually get the practice sold.

2. Walk away. This isn't a great option but many end up taking it. However, please keep in mind that *every practice* has value. Don't walk away without exploring the possibilities.

3. Hire someone to run it. This third alternative is rarely possible. If there are no buyers, chances are there are no good options for employees of this caliber. But it's worth a try.

Fortunately for accounting and tax practices there are always buyers willing to purchase—but for many sellers this requires taking off the rose-colored glasses and putting their house in order. With proper planning and assistance many difficult-to-sell practices will find suitable buyers, and the owner will be paid a fair market price. This certainly beats missed opportunities because of fear or misinformation, which can result in obtaining only a fraction of the practice value. Counting on the practice to fund your dreams of a comfortable retirement might be foolhardy, but don't walk away from a valuable asset.

What Does the Future Hold for Practice Sales?

WHAT DOES THE FUTURE HOLD FOR PRACTICE SALES?

I'm often asked about the state of the industry and what the future might hold for practice sales. My answers are always speculative, but some trends are fairly obvious.

There will always be sellers—if for no other reason than people must stop working at some point. Most of my concerns are in relation to the buyers—where will they come from? For the past 5-7 years it has been what might be described as a seller's market—that is, more buyers than sellers. I'd like to believe that a quality practice in a desirable area will always have more buyers than the selling market can satisfy, but looking at the sheer number of potential sellers should concern anyone thinking about an exit strategy in 5 plus years.

Until the time when sellers outnumber buyers in large numbers, I believe we'll see more of the same—quality practices in metro areas selling relatively quickly with rural practices taking longer—but certainly very few practitioners will walk away from their practice without a buyer.

The market won't turn overnight. We saw a slowdown starting in mid-2007 and continuing through the end of the year. It's impossible to say whether this is the beginning of some turning point or simply jitters running through the economy as a whole. My guess is jitters. We still have many more buyers than sellers in the system. If anything, a poor performing economy will force even more people into the buyer arena.

However, at some point in the future, it becomes hard to imagine enough buyers out there to satisfy the number of sellers. As the table turns we'll see prices come down and buyers will have more options. It's possible many practices won't find a buyer; at least, not in the sense that we experience today. The transition to a buyer's market will leave many sellers with very few options and possibly lead to working through the term of the real estate lease and walking away from the practice. Then again, as the buyer's market matures we'll see other types of buyers enter the field—those that see opportunity in roll ups, outsourcing, and other creative acquisition styles and operations. These buyers are starting to circle even now, but the market is not in their favor.

In short, these are service businesses with recurring revenues and will always be attractive to buyers. The unanswered question is: Who will the buyers be? It seems inevitable that a cataclysmic change is coming. Timing the market will be difficult and sellers should continue with their plans to run the practice until they are ready to retire. At that point, the market will set the price and terms, and—believe it or not—life will go on.

SHOULD I ACCEPT A LETTER OF INTENT?

SHOULD I ACCEPT A LETTER OF INTENT?

Remember, this book focuses on practices with gross revenues of up to $2 million; therefore, the answer to this question is, no. Using information provided from the seller combined with a face-to-face compatibility check, the buyer should be comfortable making an offer in the form of a final purchase agreement. Anything else is a waste of time.

A Letter of Intent often doesn't require a cash deposit, it is completely non-binding, it usually doesn't specify a timeline for due diligence or other contingencies—it misses the target entirely. Multi-million dollar homes are sold every day without an LOI; buyers complete and sign a purchase agreement that provides protection while moving the process along. An LOI doesn't work anything out beyond price, and price is only the beginning of the negotiation process. It would not serve the buyer or seller in any transaction; as far as I can tell, the only person it *would* serve is an attorney, creating unnecessary and costly billable hours.

On the other hand, a purchase agreement specifies the particulars of the transaction, prevents surprises, and can be amended when necessary. Any buyer who insists on submitting their offer as a Letter of Intent does not adequately understand the process and is almost certainly a "tire kicker".

WHO DRAFTS THE FINAL PURCHASE AGREEMENT?

WHO DRAFTS THE FINAL PURCHASE AGREEMENT?

Written offers come from the buyer. The seller has already made his offer in the form of the asking price; therefore, the buyer is responsible for drafting his offer and submitting it to the seller. It is the seller's responsibility to accept, reject or counter the offer. Countering the offer may involve additions, subtractions or a complete re-write, if necessary. A rejection can be accompanied by an explanation, asking that the contract be altered in some way by the buyer and re-submitted—an example being when a buyer's attorney gets involved and the contract is 50 pages of boilerplate, when the entire agreement can be 5 pages long.

This is the negotiation process. Getting to the point where a final purchase agreement is signed by both parties is an accomplishment. It means that the vast majority of negotiations are complete, the various details having been worked out.

What Items are Contingent in the Purchase Agreement?

WHAT ITEMS ARE CONTINGENT IN THE PURCHASE AGREEMENT?

The purchase agreement will be subject to certain conditions or contingencies. *It is important to have a timeline and expiration for each contingency*—this cannot be emphasized strongly enough. A contingency without a deadline leaves the contract open to cancellation without recourse. Each contingency should be removed individually as the requirements are met. This keeps the transaction headed in the right direction and focused on priorities. When all contingencies are satisfied, the buyer's deposit should become non-refundable, attesting to the fact that the provisions of the purchase agreement have been met and the transaction can close as scheduled.

Following are the three most common contingencies when selling a practice.

Due Diligence Contingency: The buyer's ability to perform satisfactory diligence is often extended until the day of close. This should not happen! Multiple timelines should be attached to this contingency, e.g. 5 days for the buyer to provide a list of due diligence items and 5 days for the seller to prepare/compile those items; then 15 days for the buyer's investigation, not to exceed 30 days. The contract should provide a means for the buyer to affirmatively remove the contingency at any time.

Lease Contingency: Most practices are located in leased premises. The buyer will need to speak with the landlord and either assume the current lease or secure a new lease that is satisfactory. If the seller owns the real estate and will be leasing to the buyer, a new lease will be drafted and executed. This shouldn't take more than 30 days to accomplish.

Loan Contingency: When sellers receive all cash at close, it almost always involves the buyer securing third party financing, whether that be a home equity loan or small business loan. The contract will be contingent upon loan approval. Here again, multiple timelines should be attached to this contingency, e.g. 15 days to produce a pre-qualification letter, 30 days for a loan commitment letter, then some trigger that finalizes this contingency entirely. This is a sensitive issue for most buyers. No buyer wants their deposit becoming non-refundable when the bank hasn't actually wired the money, but the money isn't usually wired until mere days before close. At some point prior to close, this contingency must be removed, and usually is in process of time; i.e. the contract says that if the buyer doesn't back out after 30 days then all contingencies are understood to be satisfied and the contract is enforceable.

Anything can be a contingency in a contract if the buyer and seller agree upon it, but these three conditions are standard for most transactions.

Should I Involve
My Attorney?

SHOULD I INVOLVE MY ATTORNEY?

Disclaimer: I am *not* an attorney. If you have legal questions please consult with a licensed attorney. This is the disclaimer I attach to every email involving legal questions. The same disclaimer applies to this book. It should probably read, "please consult with a *qualified and knowledgeable* attorney", one who has been involved with multiple practice acquisitions (good luck) or at least business sales in general.

I never discourage buyers or sellers from speaking with legal counsel, but high quality attorneys with common sense can be very difficult to find, and asking attorneys to draft a document from scratch is usually a formula for disaster. If at all possible, I recommend finalizing the document in question and then sending it to the attorney for a legal opinion. They will review a 5-page purchase agreement and always recommend changes—it's how they make a living—but this beats paying for a 50-page contract that nobody can understand. I believe it was Will Rogers who said, "The minute you read something you can't understand, you can almost be sure it was drawn up by a lawyer." I couldn't agree more!

Above all, remember your attorney works for you, not the other way around.

Does the Sale Go Through an Escrow or Closing Attorney?

DOES THE SALE GO THROUGH AN ESCROW OR CLOSING ATTORNEY?

An escrow (Closing Attorney in some states) is not required of all transactions, but if the buyer is using third party financing to purchase the practice, the bank will require it. They will not wire funds directly into the seller's account. Escrow protects the lender by performing a lien search, clearing the "title" of the assets. They also file a lien on the buyer's other assets as security for the loan (as required by the lender) and an additional lien, securing the assets of the business. When escrow is involved, the bank is assured that all the provisions of the purchase agreement are met prior to close, giving them confidence to then transfer the funds.

As you can see, escrow is really there to protect the buyer and the bank. This is true with most transactions involving property. The seller has no need for protection, he only requires that the money reach his bank account before turning over ownership. Nevertheless, buyer and seller generally split the cost of escrow.

Because tax and accounting practices don't have tangible inventory or large capital assets, a Bulk Sale is not required. This eliminates the need to publish the sale and avoids other time-consuming paper shuffling. It is important that you use a title company that is familiar with tax and accounting practice sales in order for them to understand those areas that are unique to the profession. If you have your own buyer then ask a broker for referrals to a qualified title company.

Escrow is generally opened immediately following satisfactory due diligence by the buyer.

What Options are Available in Financing a Practice?

WHAT OPTIONS ARE AVAILABLE IN FINANCING A PRACTICE?

Banks love to finance tax and accounting practice acquisitions, and since buyers usually don't have enough cash sitting around to pay 100% of the purchase price up front, this is fortunate! The default rate on these loans is one of the lowest in the industry. There are both SBA lenders and conventional lenders in this market.

Bank Loans

The primary source of cash in this industry is found in SBA guaranteed loans. SBA lenders are willing to loan based primarily on the historical cash flow of the business, the buyer's credit history, and the buyer's experience. Interest rates on these loans are reasonable, and a ten year term allows for manageable payments. The disadvantage to SBA financing can be the bureaucratic process of application and approval. It is very important that the buyer work with a specialized SBA lender; someone with experience lending to tax and accounting practices who has knowledgeable, dedicated underwriters.

Most conventional financing is difficult to obtain, owing to the bank's insistence on collateral lending, but more and more conventional lenders are springing up. Due to low default risks, conventional lenders can be competitive by mimicking the larger SBA lenders in the way they package and sell these loans. This trend seems to be accelerating, which will open up even more options for buyers and sellers in the coming years.

It must be understood that both the practice and the buyer are required to qualify for financing; in fact, it is harder to qualify the practice than the buyer. In order to meet the criteria, the practice must generate enough cash flow to cover 125% of the new owner's salary and his debt payments. Given that salary needs vary depending on obligations and other sources of income such as a spouse's earnings,

experience, and proper credentials. When the going gets tough, the buyer will step up to the plate and find a way to make the investment work, or else he will sell the practice in order to preserve his good credit and recoup as much of his investment as possible. With this knowledge, the lender can sleep in peace.

What is Included in the Sales Price of a Practice?

WHAT IS INCLUDED IN THE SALES PRICE OF A PRACTICE?

If the entire practice is for sale, then the price includes everything it takes to run the business—equipment, client lists, trade fixtures, leasehold improvements, phone numbers, business records, goodwill, trade secrets, supplies and inventory. With smaller practices, work in progress is also included in the purchase price, but given the time of year in which most practices sell, this amount is minimal. Occasionally larger practices will need to address work in progress separately. Bank accounts, cash, and accounts receivable would *not* be included. The only exception would be a stock sale, but this rarely takes place when selling practices under $2 million.

There is generally an exhibit attached to the purchase agreement that lists furniture and equipment being sold. It may also be appropriate to attach an exhibit that includes those items which will *not* be sold— personal items in the office such as art work, photos, certificates, etc.

When only a portion of a practice is being sold, a much more specific itemization is required regarding what is or is not for sale, especially if the seller plans to remain in their current location. If the seller is simply offering all of their 1040 work, a list of those clients and the associated revenue should be specified. If the seller plans to retain a large chunk of the practice, questions will arise about staff and whether they will be available to the buyer. There are also software licensing issues and other variables to consider. The entire process can be complicated and needs to be well planned and executed.

How is the
Purchase Price
Allocated?

HOW IS THE PURCHASE PRICE ALLOCATED?

The allocation of the purchase price is a major negotiation point when selling manufacturing businesses with inventory, large machinery, and vehicles. However, the allocation of tax and accounting practices is generally straightforward: 5% to FF&E; some arbitrary smallish amount to the Covenant Not to Compete, approximately $10-20K; and the balance to Goodwill. This can vary depending on the size of the practice but works well for most transactions below $2 million. Buyers and sellers used to be at odds regarding the allocation to Covenant Not to Compete, but in recent years the tax law has reduced this friction.

Regarding the Covenant Not to Compete, there are many different legal opinions on whether you must allocate to the covenant in order to make it enforceable; some say "yes" while others say "no". Those saying "yes" believe any amount protects the buyer by making the covenant enforceable. Those saying "no" believe the covenant is enforceable without the allocation, and actually stronger since the entire purchase price can be brought to bear; they argue that a smaller allocation means the seller could go compete and the only loss a buyer could claim is the amount allocated to the covenant. If you're a lawyer reading this book and can show me case law to prove one or the other, I would be interested in such information. In the meantime, we continue to allocate as described above.

WHO ARE THE BUYERS?

WHO ARE THE BUYERS?

Believe it or not, the best buyer is not a larger firm. It is usually an individual, and frequently a current employee of another practice near you. This is true for a couple of reasons. Firstly, existing firms often do not have the excess capacity in staff to handle the additional work. In a typical sale, the seller is ready to retire; at close, the buyer must be willing to assume the work load and devote time to the transition.

The reason a firm buys a practice is oftentimes different from an individual buyer's reasons; and even when they are similar, the reward for the individual buyer is greater. Firms are less motivated and less likely to carry a substantial amount of the risk involved in an acquisition, almost always insisting on a client retention agreement. When the potential buyer is an individual with several years of experience, who has dreamed of owning a practice, that buyer will be willing to bear more of the financial risk and assume greater responsibility of client transition.

The best buyer for a practice grossing $2 million or less is an individual. They are motivated to pay a fair market price on terms acceptable to the seller and they also have the time and energy to complete a smooth transition. The clients are happier because they go from one owner-operator to another—after all, who wants to talk to a staff member when they are accustomed to dealing with the owner? When you hear about clients leaving en masse after the sale of a practice, it is because it was sold to a large firm and the clients were shuffled off to an unknown staff person. How would *you* feel? The purchasing firm isn't concerned because they will only pay a percentage of gross collected; and when there is no client, there is no gross collected.

The very best buyers are experienced individuals who currently work for someone else. They are fed up with being an employee and want to work for themselves. The next best buyer is a sole proprietor with a small practice who wants to take it to the next level. They realize it's much easier to purchase an existing practice than slowly build up the clientele via referrals and marketing. These small practice owners will often step up and compete with individual buyers. Occasionally, a large firm will become sufficiently motivated to step up and compete with individual buyers, but it is a rare occurrence when they are willing to pay the same price, under the same terms, as a buyer who is purchasing a job.

How Does One Effectively Find a Buyer?

HOW DOES ONE EFFECTIVELY FIND A BUYER?

Sellers who desire strong offers from quality buyers must be willing to spend heavily on marketing. There must also be a system in place for weeding through the various buyers who respond. Sellers often ask where I will be advertising their practice. Aside from our proprietary website, a seller can advertise everywhere I advertise; assuming they are willing to spend several thousand dollars a month and some substantial upfront costs on ad development. Experience has shown even this isn't enough, since it takes time for buyers to respond to the marketing message. That being said, a practice in a good location will attract buyer inquiries regardless.

The more important question is whether a seller really wants to take the calls that result from proper marketing, and whether they have a system for qualifying the buyers. (See next question *"How are buyers pre-qualified?"*) If not, they will become extremely frustrated. At any given time, there are thousands of buyers actively looking at practices for sale. For every thousand prospective buyers, there may be only 40-50 of them who are qualified and properly motivated. A person could run their practice into the ground while scrambling for the time to sift through the unqualified buyers; which explains why many sellers choose to hire a specialized broker to manage the madness!

How are Buyers Pre-Qualified?

HOW ARE BUYERS PRE-QUALIFIED?

Having a system in place is necessary to filter through the serious buyer inquiries and determine who is actually qualified and who is not. This system also plays a role in keeping the sale of a practice confidential. Confidentiality prevents employees, competitors, and staff from becoming alarmed by the sale, ensuring that they be informed properly and when the time is right.

Every buyer should provide the following items prior to meeting the seller.

Confidentiality Agreement: This agreement should be specific to the state in which the practice is located and should give the seller every legal avenue possible to protect their confidentiality, should the buyer choose to breach this trust.

Financial Statement: Special consideration should be taken regarding the buyer's available cash on hand. If the buyer is drawing from home equity to produce the cash then an explanation should be obtained as to when this will take place and whether they are pre-qualified to borrow the needed funds. Cash is king—any arbitrary explanation as to where they are coming up with the funds is worthless. *Rule of Thumb:* When the buyer tells you his amount of money to invest *"depends on the deal"*, it means he doesn't have any money of his own.

Credit Report: This can be obtained prior to meeting, or at the time an offer is presented, and is necessary to confirm creditworthiness. Whether a seller is considering carrying the note or there will be third-party financing, authorization should be signed prior to a meeting taking place.

Résumé: A full résumé or even a brief biography says a lot about a buyer and his experience in the field. Many buyers haven't prepared a résumé for a decade or more, having worked for the same employer the entire time. The care they take in providing this information says much about them.

Important Questions: Important questions that affect the buyer's ability to secure financing should be posed prior to meeting the seller, such as: Have you ever filed bankruptcy? Have you ever been arrested or convicted of a felony? Are you on parole? *It Happens!* SBA will not lend to someone that is on parole, regardless of the reason.

Qualifying buyers is a full-time job when performed properly and involves more than simply having the paperwork in order. Buyers will give many telltale signs along the way that will qualify or disqualify them depending on the situation. Remember that the buyer will be asked to take on some heavy commitments, but before those take place plenty of smaller ones come along. Often it is how they handle the smaller commitments that will determine the future. The right buyer will be enthusiastic, cooperative and willing to pay fair market value. Somewhere along the line the flakes will reveal themselves. Whether doing it yourself or hiring a broker, be certain proper guidelines are followed to ensure your best interest.

SHOULD THE BUYER WORK IN THE PRACTICE PRIOR TO CLOSE?

SHOULD THE BUYER WORK IN THE PRACTICE PRIOR TO CLOSE?

Once a buyer and seller have agreed on price and signed the purchase agreement, a temptation to have the buyer work in the practice starts to arise because both parties are eager to begin their new lives. The buyer may feel this is a good time to begin working in the practice and the seller is happy to have the buyer's assistance. However, there are a lot of details to work out prior to close. This is a dramatic change for both parties and tensions can run high.

The process can and sometimes does drag on for months. Many things can cause a delay, and even when every "t" is crossed and every "i" is dotted, the buyer and seller may find themselves waiting the last couple weeks for the lender to fund. I have found that once a buyer is actively working in the practice, he or she is no longer as motivated to finalize the sale.

Sometimes a buyer with early possession will begin to question the purchase; or at times the seller begins to doubt the buyer's ability to run the practice. You may also begin having problems with employees who don't have a clear idea of who is in charge. The buyer may want to initiate changes which are in conflict with your current management style, and confusion in the staff can lead to severe problems. For these reasons and many more, employing the buyer prior to close should be avoided, if at all possible.

There are some obvious exceptions. For instance, the buyer may already work there and is known and accepted by their colleagues. Even then, you may want to wait until after close before announcing the sale to the rest of the staff. Occasionally the timing necessitates some form of early possession. For instance, if a transaction was scheduled to close February 15, all contingencies had been removed and the buyer's down payment had become non-refundable, the buyer and seller may feel it would be best if the buyer began meeting clients to initiate the transition. These sorts of scheduling crises should be avoided if possible, but sometimes health or other concerns force the issue. Every transaction is different and requires its own judgments as it pertains to early possession.

WHAT QUESTIONS WILL A SELLER BE ASKED?

WHAT QUESTIONS WILL A SELLER BE ASKED?

Sellers will be asked different questions at different points in the process. Brokers have questions, buyers have questions and then due diligence, banks have questions, landlords have questions, and so on. Most questions are not difficult to answer. For starters, sellers should be able to answer the following questions for anyone that might ask:

Please tell me a little about your practice. This means what type of services are provided, how many clients you serve, what your billing rates are, the history of your clientele, etc.?

Why do you want to sell? The answer may be simple or complex. If the seller is 65 years old, qualifies for Medicare, and has been in public accounting for 40 years, retirement is an easy answer. But if the seller is in their forties and doesn't have a concrete reason for selling other than burn out, this will concern buyers. Buyers will wonder why someone would sell such a wonderful practice! Selling the practice to take advantage of a job opportunity or because of health problems may be a good reason to sell, but selling without any logical explanation is not.

What are your plans after you sell? If retirement, will the seller be staying in the area? If a job opportunity, where and when will this take place? Often times, this question gets asked to confirm a seller's reason for selling and put this subject to rest.

Tell me about your employees. The seller should be familiar with the amount of time each employee has worked there, their approximate ages, and educational levels. Does any staff represent a competition risk to the buyer? Are long term employees nearing retirement themselves? Do any aspire to be the buyer?

What kind of clients do you have? Some practices are easier than others to describe. Try to keep it short without leaving out important items. Is there any concentration in the client base, i.e. 70% are in construction, 40% only speak Korean, the top two clients represent 20% of gross revenue? Consider what would be important if you were asking this question.

What is your description of the perfect buyer? The answer should come quickly and include more than "a buyer with cash". What kind of personality, experience and age range would appeal best to your clients?

What are your expectations of a broker? Is it simply to bring a buyer to the table? Is it to negotiate the best price? To make sure things are done in an orderly fashion? The answers will determine how you proceed with a broker and what follow-up questions to ask.

If a seller is serious about selling their practice and doing it right, they should be prepared to answer these basic questions and others that will come along. None of them are particularly difficult, but it's best to be prepared and orderly rather than hesitant and unsure.

What Should be Included in Letters to Clients?

WHAT SHOULD BE INCLUDED IN LETTERS TO CLIENTS?

Whether the buyer and seller send separate letters or one joint letter, the following examples should come in handy. It would also be a nice touch for the buyer to include a résumé, with the format catering to professionals and non-professionals alike; the buyer can then reinforce this information when calling the client.

Below are two sample letters which may be helpful. If you would like copies in MS Word, feel free to email me at *roy@questbrokers.com* and ask about sample introduction letters. We have many versions for different circumstances.

Seller Sample:

Dear _____:

For the last several months I have diligently pondered my future and that of my family. I have enjoyed public accounting for over __ years and I have made the decision to retire. I have many dear clients whom I have enjoyed serving over the years. In coming to the decision to retire I have meticulously searched for an individual who is competent, knowledgeable, and skilled in taxation, accounting and auditing. (Buyer) is such a man.

(Buyer) will assume all of my tax, accounting, and audit clients and will move into and establish his offices where my office has been, (Address). The phone numbers, as well as the staff, will remain the same and your files will be here, as always.

(Buyer) has been involved in public accounting for a number of years in (County). He is a graduate of _____ University and holds a Master's Degree in taxation from _____ University. He is also a Certified QuickBooks Professional Advisor.

I am confident your tax, accounting, and audit needs will be well taken care of and the high-quality service you are now accustomed to will continue. If you have any questions at all, please give him the opportunity to address them.

Sincerely,

(Seller)

Buyer Sample:

Dear _____:

I have been asked by (Seller) to take over your tax and accounting needs. I just wanted to welcome you and let you know how pleased I am for this opportunity to be of service to you.

(Seller), as you might expect, is intent on ensuring this transition is smooth, with little or no inconvenience to you. To accomplish this, (Seller) and I have taken the following steps:

1. We have reviewed your tax records that will remain at the current location, where they will be readily available in case of government inquiry, loan verification, tax consultation, etc.

2. We have assigned you a preferential pre-scheduled appointment before my calendar begins to fill. You, of course, may change the appointment if it is not convenient. We have attempted to make it as close to last year's appointment as possible.

3. I have reviewed (Seller)'s fee schedule as well and found it to be similar to those of our firm. Unless there are some special circumstances, you can expect the fees to be essentially the same.

4. (Seller) will be available to this office for any questions that may arise concerning past returns, in case of government inquiry or audit.

5. I will make myself available, either by phone or by appointment, to meet with you prior to your tax appointment so we can get to know each other in advance. Should you need year-end tax planning, as many do with the new law changes, I will be happy to schedule an appointment with you.

We want the transition to be pleasant and comfortable for you. If there is anything you need or something we can help you with, please call. We are here to help.

You have also been placed on our newsletter mailing list and your first issue will arrive (date). I look forward to serving you!

Sincerely,

(Buyer)

How Does My Existing Real Estate Lease Affect the Sale?

HOW DOES MY EXISTING REAL ESTATE LEASE AFFECT THE SALE?

The number of potential buyers is a direct reflection of practice value. The more buyers there are, the better price and terms when the practice sells. Thus, it is important to understand how the real estate lease affects various buyers, and why.

Many buyers already own a small practice of their own and are prepared to take it to the next level by purchasing another practice. Unlike larger firms, these buyers will pay cash and are motivated similarly to individual buyers that have never owned a practice. However, these buyers are often behind a lease of their own and cannot assume your existing lease. Other buyers want longevity in location and insist on assuming your existing lease—when a bank is involved, they will require a long term lease as a prerequisite of lending. The key in regard to your lease is flexibility—the ability to exit your existing lease at or close to the time of sale, or assurance that the landlord will extend a long term lease to a qualified buyer.

There are some remedies that can be applied to lease issues. Perhaps your existing space could be sub-leased; or if you're losing your lease, some specific thought could be put into the best site available for relocation. If your landlord refuses to sign a long term lease—*these landlords do exist*—then this can be addressed up front and dealt with accordingly.

There are other issues surrounding the lease, such as a practice bulging at the seams. It is an exceptional buyer that would be willing to move the practice to larger premises while at the same time transitioning into the practice. On the other hand, there may be a practice which has shrunk over the years and now occupies much more space than is needed. Either way, there are various remedies that can be applied, depending on the location and the market for buyers.

The bottom line is, flexibility is paramount. If you're up against a lease that is expiring, try to go month-to-month, or sign a short term lease if necessary. Obviously you don't want your lease to expire in March, but signing that new 5 year lease could make the sale of your practice impractical to many highly qualified buyers. Informing the landlord of plans to turn over the practice to a new owner often works well. They may be willing to go short term with the understanding that the buyer will have interest in signing a new long term lease prior to close—something that might be more favorable to the landlord than what you're willing to commit to.

I Own the Building; Can I Sell or Lease it?

I Own the Building; Can I Sell or Lease it?

Many configurations are possible, but it is important to consider how it affects the number of potential buyers. If selling the practice and real estate together, there will be far fewer buyers to work with (this can approach zero buyers depending on the cost of the real estate and whether it has tenants other than you). There may be several buyers interested if you're the only tenant and the real estate is priced fairly.

Sellers who own their building should charge themselves market rent for at least three years prior to the sale. Otherwise, it will be necessary to adjust the financials in order to reflect a reasonable rental expense which the buyer will incur. The buyer's net income from the practice will not match the seller's net income if market rent is three times as much as shown on the seller's financials. A higher market rent will increase the value of the real estate and, at the same time, typically lower the value of the practice.

If you're able to sell the real estate for market value only given a large rent increase, the above still holds true. The seller may be charging himself $2,000 a month for a building that's worth $950,000. Nobody is purchasing a building for this amount in order to collect $24,000 a year in rent; the rent must be increased to justify the building's value. That increase will lower the net income of the practice and could make it impossible for the practice to make a profit. If the building has been appreciating and rent has not been adjusted properly over the years, the seller may have no choice but to sell the practice and real estate separately, in which case they must be prepared to offer the premises for lease on a short-term basis and at an affordable rate. This will allow the buyer time to transition before finding a new space to lease.

WHAT HAPPENS IF I DIE AT MY DESK?

WHAT HAPPENS IF I DIE AT MY DESK?

Obviously this question is most pertinent to sole practitioners, but it can concern partnerships as well. Depending on the time of year and the heir's ability to move in a timely fashion, the transfer of a practice can still take place.

At one time, an owner passed away in October and his sister called me in February wanting to salvage the practice value. Of course, all the bookkeeping clients had left and tax season was under way. Contrast that with the wife who calls two weeks after her husband's passing, and we receive full value for the practice. I've followed up with mourning relatives to see if there was any way I could be of assistance, only to find they are calling every client and asking them to come pick up their file; unaware that there was substantial value to the practice.

It is important to make sure beneficiaries know who to call, should the sole proprietor pass away or fall ill. They should be aware of the value of the practice and of the importance of timing. Many owners find the easiest thing to do is write a short letter and include it with their will or living trust documents. Giving a copy to a trusted employee can be even more effective, or at least asking them to direct the heirs to instructions within the estate documents, should something happen.

Many owners ask about this subject. For a copy of a Codicil to Will document that works well, email me at: *roy@questbrokers.com.*

When Should I Tell My Staff About the Sale?

When Should I Tell My Staff About the Sale?

There are really only two viable options when it comes to announcing the sale to your staff. The first is not telling them until after the transaction closes; and the second is telling them immediately after the decision to sell has been made, before a buyer has been secured. There are a few variations, but these are the general choices.

After close: You gather everyone together and tell them you've sold. If handled properly, this is the best way to go, both for you and the buyer. Assure them that you've found a perfect replacement and that the new owner intends to keep everything the same, including retaining all the staff. Be prepared to answer questions, mostly to soothe anxieties they may have. The staff will be upset at first and some will handle it better than others. Calm their fears with honesty, but remember that most people react emotionally. Have the new owner in there as soon as possible, no more than a couple of days. This gives people less time to worry about the initial meeting. Once they've met the new owner and see the interaction with clients, they will accept the change and move on. It's now up to the buyer to continue making a good impression and taking on the leadership role in the practice.

Prior to close: This method is not recommended unless completely necessary. For instance, you may be located in an area that makes it impossible to market your practice without everyone knowing. The good news is that practices in this situation are often in smaller rural areas and the employees have fewer options for employment. Even then, it is best to postpone the announcement as long as possible, leaving the employees less time for fear to set in—fear of change, fear of the new owner's arrival, etc. Staff members may begin looking for new jobs because they are uncertain about their current employment. Even when they stay they can begin resenting you for your decision and cause transition problems down the road.

There are many opinions on this subject and every practice is a little different. It may be appropriate to have the new owner in the announcement meeting immediately following close. It could make sense to tell a key employee about the sale prior to close, but not the remainder of the staff. Knowing the right move takes experience that many sellers haven't had; so, as a general rule of thumb, don't tell anyone that you're selling until the transaction closes.

Why Should I Hire a Broker?

WHY SHOULD I HIRE A BROKER?

It's more interesting to begin by asking: Can a practice be sold without the use of a broker? The undisputed answer is obviously yes. I imagine most practices still sell through private parties. These transactions invariably involve 100% revenue guarantees and small or no down payment to the seller. The deal may spell out 100% of gross revenue as the sale price, but since the seller bears all the risk of client retention and the buyer has little or no motivation to retain unpleasant clients, the final score is 70-80% of gross. If this appeals to a seller, they may not need a broker! Anyone looking to purchase would have interest in these terms. All it would take is a phone call or an e-mail to the practices in that area.

Sellers hire brokers because they believe the broker will do a better job than they would. Knowing whether the broker you're hiring has any practical experience and any success selling practices in your area—*that's the hard part!*

Key functions of a broker

Practice valuation: Fair market value is what a willing buyer will pay a willing seller, period. Without selling a number of practices in a particular area, a broker couldn't possibly know what fair market value is for the practice. Without this experience it's simply theory. The right broker will know the value based on experience.

Confidentiality: Brokers protect the seller and buyer in every possible way, even though the selling process requires the sharing of information. Using a good broker is the optimal way to ensure confidentiality.

Packaging and marketing: Quality brokers have expertise and know what makes a firm attractive to a buyer. They can therefore identify strong selling points for each practice, which a seller might not have considered.

Finding prospective buyers: Brokers should be constantly marketing to buyers through state and chapter publications, websites, direct mail, phone solicitation, and trade shows. This results in a large database of interested buyers of all sorts.

Buyer qualification: Brokers screen prospective buyers in several ways. They obtain documents such as credit reports and financial statements, as well as interview buyers regarding credentials and experience. Sellers do not want to waste time with buyers who may not be qualified or serious. (See *"How are buyers pre-qualified?"*)

Consultation: A broker works with owners throughout the process regarding all aspects of the sale, including the terms of sale, financing issues, non-compete and other contract issues, client retention, and whatever else is needed to make the process run smoothly.

Negotiations: Brokers provide important third-party negotiation skills to ensure that the deal gets done under terms that are satisfactory. This is one of the most underappreciated aspects of what a good broker provides and could fill an entire book of its own. This is where the broker either pays for himself or costs the seller money.

Financing: Large brokerage firms have access and expertise in obtaining financing for the buyer so that the seller can receive cash at close if the practice and buyer qualify. (See *"What options are available in financing a practice?"*) A broker can also provide guidance and valuable experience with regard to seller financing issues when necessary.

Large Pools of Buyers: It is simple Economics 101: Sellers can't get the best deal from one or two potential buyers they met at the CPE seminar. The larger the pool of potential buyers, the better the chance of getting not only the right price and terms, but the best fit for your clients and staff.

There is a reason some brokers sell hundreds of practices each year, while others sell a half dozen. Some work hard and produce results while others merely list practices and wait. Selling a practice is not a simple process. It's a complex, legally binding transaction with potential repercussions far into the future.

WHAT IS THE BROKER'S COMMISSION?

WHAT IS THE BROKER'S COMMISSION?

The industry standard is 10-15% of the sales price, but can be more on smaller practices where brokers charge a minimum fee. Never list with a broker who asks for any type of upfront payment, regardless of the reason; they obviously don't have buyers and make their money selling valuations, or something along those lines.

Be suspicious of any broker charging less than 10%—it means he's struggling to get listings and probably has no experience in this specialized niche. It also signals an inability to spend the amount of money needed to find quality buyers. (See *"How does one effectively find a buyer?"*)

Above all, stay focused on the important part—the amount of money you receive *after commission*. Selling for 1.3 times gross revenue with all cash at close and no revenue guarantee, but a commission of 20%, might be preferable to selling on complete contingency payments over 5 years, but with no commission. The important question is whether the broker's commission is value added or an unnecessary expense.

The vast majority of the time the seller who uses a specialized broker will come away from the sale having been less involved in marketing and qualifying buyers, and will end up with 10-20% more money in their pocket even after paying the broker's commission.

Occasionally sellers will ask the broker to reduce their fee. It's only human.

Some advice: *Go for it!* The worst case scenario is a reply of "no". But consider this; if the broker can't negotiate *his own commission*, do you really want him negotiating the sale of your practice? So, ask away, but if the broker willingly lowers their commission below the industry standard then you should consider working with another broker.

Should I Employ a Broker if I Already Have the Buyer?

SHOULD I EMPLOY A BROKER IF I ALREADY HAVE THE BUYER?

Specialized brokers bring much more to the table than finding the buyer. They are familiar with the proper procedures involved in a successful start-to-finish acquisition. If a quality buyer is standing by but the seller needs assistance completing the transaction, hiring a broker for guidance through the land mines is advisable. Specialized brokers will charge a flat fee for services rendered which will vary depending on the amount of work you want the broker to provide.

Services Available

Valuation: Both parties usually agree that everything needs to be fair, but it is sometimes difficult to determine what a fair agreement looks like. A broker can suggest various options on price and terms, helping the buyer and seller feel equally comfortable with their decision. In this case, the broker isn't necessarily striving for fair market value (that is difficult to determine without multiple buyers), but is assisting with options that may not be readily apparent.

Negotiation: The negotiations may be minimal, but there are still points of contention that would be better handled by a broker, even if the buyer is an employee, close friend, or family member.

Purchase Agreement: A purchase agreement is necessary to spell out the terms. A good source would be a broker who consistently sells practices in your area. There are very few attorneys who specialize in business sales and almost none who have specific tax and accounting practice experience. There's a huge difference between asking an attorney to draft a purchase agreement from scratch (resulting in 40-50 pages of boilerplate that no one can understand) versus handing an attorney a specialized purchase agreement for their legal review.

Other Contracts: The same broker will have contingency removal forms that coincide with the purchase agreement, along with other necessary items, i.e. Promissory Note, Bill of Sale, etc.

Letter to Clients: Both parties could draft an appropriate letter to clients announcing the sale, but a broker should have multiple sample letters that have been fine-tuned over the years. (See *"What should be included in letters to clients?"*)

Financing: A broker can refer the buyer to an appropriate lender for financing—someone with experience financing tax and accounting practices. He can also suggest various forms of seller financing and the steps that should be taken to qualify the buyer.

The list goes on and on, from assisting with the assumption of leased premises, to employment agreements with staff, to appropriate pay levels for a seller who is staying on with the firm. It makes good business sense to have someone available who has gone through this process before. A professional broker in the field of tax and accounting practices should be willing to help without insisting on his normal commission rate. It's a small world and these transactions lead to referrals down the road.

Do Brokers Give Referrals?

DO BROKERS GIVE REFERRALS?

A broker should be able to provide referrals to both buyers and sellers. Naturally, the referrals will be positive and be of little worth other than to confirm that the broker has actually sold a practice before. I've never placed much weight on referrals, but here are some for review:

"Anything can happen when you initiate the sale of your business! I'm sure glad Roy was there to pick me up when I thought all was lost. SBA can really make you jump through hoops. With years of experience dealing with similar transactions, Roy Braatz had a trick up his sleeve for every obstacle SBA put in front of me. I would definitely use him again!"
Tom Carroll CPA – Mill Valley, CA (Seller)

"Before meeting with Roy Braatz, I believed I would only get one times gross plus have to provide revenue guarantees and terms. Boy was I wrong! All cash up front, no guarantees and I walked away with far more than expected. They did most of the work and are well worth their fee."
Lee T. Reams EA – Agoura Hills CA (Seller)
Note: I also appreciate Lee's review of this book.

"I purchased a practice along with the building and thanks to the banker that works closely with Roy and Jake, my perception of going the SBA route has changed. If you have the right people in place, obtaining the financing is a piece of cake."
Michael Hasan CPA – Vista, CA (Buyer)

"Every year, the number of deals that Roy puts together in California grows. Having handled escrow for many of those deals, we appreciate the way he conducts business. Considering the consistent manner in which they handle their clients, serving them is a pleasure."
William H. Dunn, Attorney at Law – Campbell, CA (Escrow Services)

"Roy and Jake are the reason I was able to grow my practice at a rate much faster than traditional marketing. I didn't realize buying a practice could be this "stress free". Throughout the process, Roy Braatz was there to make sure things were done right every step of the way. When it comes time to expand again, we will definitely look to these guys for opportunities!"
Kevin Ebenhoch CPA – Sherman Oaks, CA (Buyer)

"We didn't know where to find a buyer! A local firm made an offer but we really didn't want to be tied to the practice through a guarantee arrangement. The call from Roy came just in time and as a result, we were able to sell for all cash and retire care free!"
Dale & Mary Fender EA – Napa, CA (Seller)

"We needed to move quickly as David's health declined. There to help us out were Roy and Jake. Honestly, we were skeptical at first. We never thought we would collect our full value in cash at close. However, out of desperation, we took a leap of faith and they really came through for us just in time!"
Janet Briggs – San Fernando, CA (Seller)

Why Would I Pay All Cash at Close for a Practice?

WHY WOULD I PAY ALL CASH AT CLOSE FOR A PRACTICE?

Quality practices in desirable locations attract hundreds of buyers. Within this group exist a number of buyers who understand the risks involved in purchasing a practice and are willing to step up and pay all cash at close with no revenue guarantee. If they ever hope to purchase a nice practice, they know this is the price to be paid. It's not the broker who sets the fair market value—it's the market of motivated buyers. Waiting for an uninformed seller to present his practice at below market value is a futile endeavor; unless the buyer knows the seller, it will sell to someone else.

Another reason buyers pay all cash is the attractive financing available in today's market. There was a time when seller financing was the only option. Sellers required at least 20% down, or sometimes even 50%. This limited the buyers to those with cash on hand and also limited the size of practice a qualified buyer could purchase. There are now banks standing in line to lend 100% of the purchase price. With good credit, the buyer needs no assets whatsoever! A buyer with experience and good credit can purchase a $650,000 practice with no money out of pocket—the bank will even lend working capital as needed. While some buyers may hesitate to pay all cash at close, others see a huge opportunity to advance their career.

I've had sellers insist on taking 20% down and carrying a note, only to end up taking all cash because the best buyer didn't have 20% down, but they could finance the entire deal and pay cash. These loans are generally fully amortized over 10 years. Quality practices net somewhere in the neighborhood of 40-50% of gross. Buyers do the math and realize that even if they were to lose a few clients in transition, they would still come out way ahead.

WHAT TYPE OF AN OFFER SHOULD I MAKE AND WHEN?

WHAT TYPE OF AN OFFER SHOULD I MAKE AND WHEN?

Once the buyer has reviewed the details of the practice, explored compatibility via a face to face meeting with the seller, and has a solid understanding regarding the details of the practice, the next step is to make an offer. Once the offer is accepted, the buyer will move forward with due diligence, validating their understanding of the practice.

As covered in the question, *"Should I accept a Letter of Intent?"*, a final purchase agreement is the most effective form of an offer. This shows the buyer has considered the details, is serious, and ready to move.

The offer should be presented after the buyer has a clear understanding of the practice, but before detailed due diligence. This prevents the seller from conducting due diligence with multiple buyers, including some who would later make unacceptable offers. Submitting an offer prior to due diligence also saves the buyer valuable time. (See *"Why is there no detailed due diligence prior to my offer?"*)

Will the Seller Take Less Than the Asking Price?

WILL THE SELLER TAKE LESS THAN THE ASKING PRICE?

We have all been told there is no such thing as a stupid question. Well, whoever coined that phrase was wrong.

Don't ever ask a broker if the seller will accept less than the asking price; it is a stupid question. Make your best offer; then, see how the seller reacts.

The only acceptable way to ask this question is in the form of an offer. When the seller knows who the buyer is, understands their background, future plans for the practice, transition expectations, and all the other aspects of the offer, then the seller can answer this question with some confidence. Otherwise, the answer will always be, "It depends," followed by a feeling of mistrust that the buyer is simply trying to cheat the seller out of their carefully developed practice.

Why Should I Buy a Practice Rather than Build One?

WHY SHOULD I BUY A PRACTICE RATHER THAN BUILD ONE?

Assuming a quality practice is available in your area of interest, the purchase of an existing practice makes much more sense than starting from scratch. There are many explanations as to why this is true, the most important being the immediate cash flow to the buyer. Take any practice with a 40-50% net income to the owner. The buyer comes up with a 0-20% down payment and finances the balance, fully amortized over 10 years. Interest rates fluctuate so they won't be quoted here, but you may safely calculate it at two percent over the prime rate. Now deduct the yearly debt service from the net income and the remainder is available for the buyer's new salary and benefits. You will find that many practices for sale are too good to pass up!

Other benefits of purchasing a practice include an established infrastructure of clients, employees, location, equipment, software— you name it. There will be no need to guess at the efficiency with which this infrastructure is utilized because it will be reflected in the net income. Given a buyer's ability to finance the majority of the practice, is there any question that this option is cheaper in the long run than starting from rock bottom? Even if a buyer pays a premium price, they at least know what they're getting themselves into, which is not the case in many startup situations.

When the long-term prospects of the practice are in sync with your goals the purchase of an existing practice can be a very smart move! Asking the right questions can certainly help narrow the search and make the process more enjoyable. This book wasn't intended as a buyer's guide, but following are some items to consider.

Location: Or, should I say, location, location, location! I can't imagine the location being any less important than it would be purchasing a home. For many, the community in which they work is that same community in which they live. Does the location present the lifestyle you desire? Would you pay 20% more for the same practice if it were 5 minutes from your home? Do you see yourself in a Class-A building? Do you see a quaint office in a converted residential-turned-commercial area? What's happening in the community? Is it on the rise or decline? Decide where you're willing to purchase a practice or where you'd be willing to relocate in order to own the perfect practice. Then, start your search.

Fee Structure: The difference between two practices, one with low fees and the other with high fees, can be significant. There are many variables at play. Are you comfortable working with high net worth clients and advising them on tax strategies and business concerns they may have? Or would a basic 1040 practice be more in line with your skill set? Are fees high or low for the given area and type of work involved? Could fees be raised over time without losing clients? When you purchase a practice you're buying an income stream. Your ability to earn a good income will depend on the practice you purchase and the acquisition loan payments. Are you comfortable with a practice netting 20% that you can pick up cheap, knowing that you would be able to turn it around in 6-12 months and bring the net up to 50%?

Client Type: What kind of work do you prefer doing? This often ties into fee structure, but not always. Some practices only do business returns and all personal returns are done elsewhere; this presents a huge "up side" for any buyer willing to take on personal returns. Some practices are tax only and there's an opportunity to add bookkeeping and other services. Buyers need to exercise some flexibility when looking at the client types and the makeup of a particular practice, also taking into consideration what the practice could become with some focus from a new owner. As retirees, many sellers have not marketed their practices for 20+ years. There are many diamonds in the rough—profitable practices which could be even more profitable with a younger energetic buyer at the helm!

Real Estate Lease Terms: Lease terms are much less critical in tax and accounting than they are in restaurants and other location-specific businesses. However, they still carry some importance for a number of reasons. If the seller has a few years remaining on the lease, it must be assumed by the buyer. This eliminates buyers who already have a practice and a lease of their own, and had planned to bring the practices together. On the flip side, if the seller's office space isn't available for rent, the buyer must look at moving the practice. This turns off buyers that wanted longevity in location and have no interest in hunting for new space. There are solutions such as sub-leasing the space or having the seller move the practice prior to close. As mentioned, these variables aren't as critical in practice sales, but certainly warrant some attention. (See *"How does my existing real estate lease affect the sale?"*)

The *ideal opportunity* is in the eye of the beholder, but asking the right questions about your needs and desires for purchasing a practice is a good starting point. This will eliminate a lot of frustration and help to avoid the common mistakes buyers make when purchasing an existing practice.

Why is There No Detailed Due Diligence Prior to My Offer?

WHY IS THERE NO DETAILED DUE DILIGENCE PRIOR TO MY OFFER?

I have answered this question indirectly in other areas of the book, but it's a common question and should be addressed more specifically. Remember that this book is intended for practices grossing $2 million or less. Larger practices may require more extensive diligence before a realistic offer can be tendered. With smaller practices however (especially those involving one owner), an offer should be forthcoming after the presentation of a practice summary that includes those items outlined in the chapter, *"What should be provided to the buyer prior to the first meeting?"*.

Why would further details be withheld until after an acceptable offer is presented? Because there is a definite distinction between that information used to *decide* about making an offer and that used to *verify* the facts you were given. It is reasonable to see financials prior to your offer since this will be used as part of your basis for creating the offer, but it is unnecessary to view bank statements at that point; the financials would presumably be correct. There are essentially three reasons a seller doesn't want to jump into full-blown due diligence prior to an acceptable offer:

1. The seller doesn't want everyone that expresses interest in the practice to have admittance to these personal details. Nearby competitors and others not intending to purchase the practice would have access to sensitive information.

2. It's a complete waste of time going into due diligence with a buyer that hasn't committed to making an offer. Due diligence can be a significant time burden on the seller, who must simultaneously continue to operate the practice.

3. Due diligence may involve information that reveals client names and other confidential information in which access should be minimized.

Due diligence, after acceptance of the offer, is the buyer's opportunity to review all material facts regarding the purchase, in order to confirm that what they were told was correct. If due diligence were to reveal differences that would have affected the buyer's original offer, the buyer would then have the opportunity to retract the offer or to make a new one based on the information presented. Unlike most business sales, the due diligence portion of a tax and accounting practice transaction is a smooth process with very few surprises.

To put it simply, due diligence is not the period of time for a buyer to decide whether or not to continue with the purchase. That decision, including price and terms, is made at the time of the offer. The purpose of due diligence is to verify information.

WHAT SERVICES CAN A BROKER OFFER TO BUYERS?

WHAT SERVICES CAN A BROKER OFFER TO BUYERS?

Specialized brokers have the practices you want to buy. Waiting on a *For Sale by Owner* to materialize in your area could take months or even years, and gauging a seller's intentions and motivation for selling can be quite difficult. Quality brokers don't waste time on unattractive listings, so most of the sellers that are "just thinking about selling" have been weeded out.

The general outline of the buying process is often of interest to many buyers:

1. The buyer submits information to become registered to review a current listing and/or be notified of future opportunities.

2. The broker then works together with the buyer to find a practice that fits their requirements.

3. Once the right practice is found, the buyer meets with the seller to gain further insight about the policies, procedures, and operations of the practice.

4. If the practice continues to be of interest, the broker will assist in submitting an offer. This offer is contingent on due diligence.

5. The broker continues to assist with financing options and other items as needed, making sure the buyer is able to fulfill the requirements of the purchase agreement.

6. Finally, the broker works with both parties to set a close date, assuring that everything is in place as needed, and securing a successful transaction.

Sellers generally do not bear the risk of client retention. Ultimately, buyers should take control over client satisfaction and practices should not be sold under any type of "seller guarantee" or pricing formula based on the buyer's success. Most practices will be sold for all cash at close or with a note that is fixed in its amount and is not contingent on the future success of the buyer. If a seller desires to make an exception to this general principal, the buyer will be informed by the broker. (See *Who bears the risk of client retention?*)

This may not answer all your questions about the buying process. Feel free to contact me with any questions you may have at *roy@ questbrokers.com.*